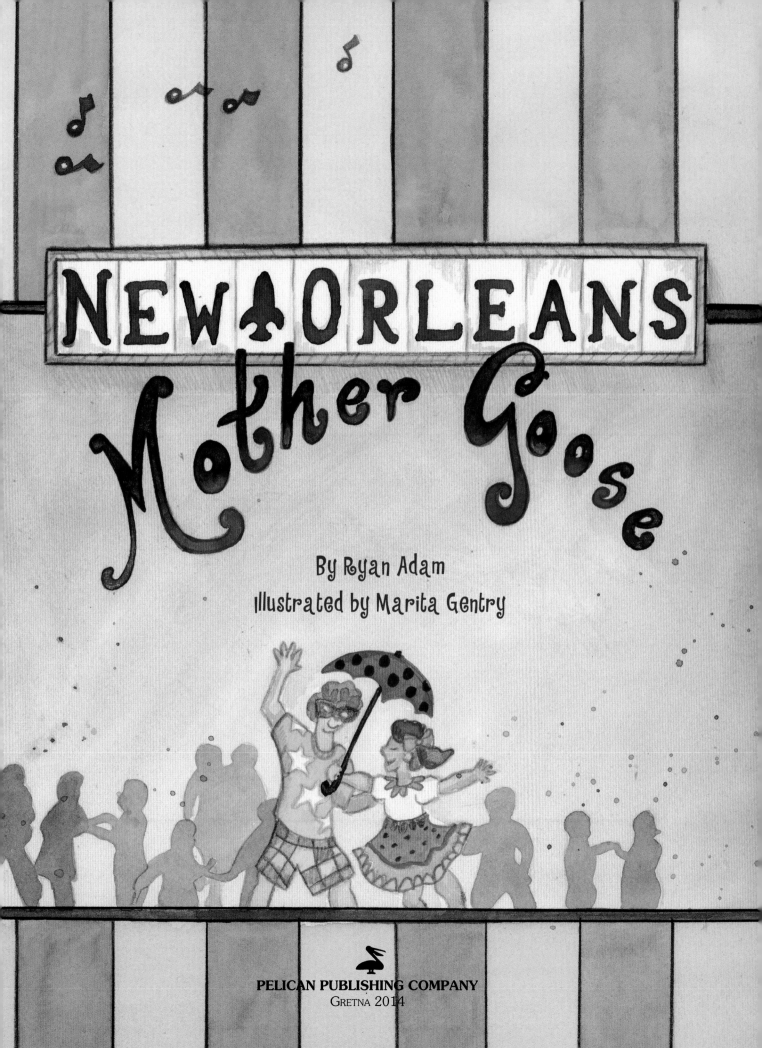

NEW ORLEANS Mother Goose

By Ryan Adam

Illustrated by Marita Gentry

PELICAN PUBLISHING COMPANY

Gretna 2014

To three beautiful women in my life: my grandmother, Rose Duplantis; my godmother,
Lyla Buquet; and, especially, my mother, JoAnne Duplantis—R. A.

First printing, September 2014
Second printing, February 2018

The word "Pelican" and the depiction of a pelican are
trademarks of Pelican Publishing Company, Inc., and are
registered in the U.S. Patent and Trademark Office.

Library of Congress Cataloging-in-Publication Data

Adam, Ryan, author.
    New Orleans Mother Goose / by Ryan Adam ; illustrated by Marita Gentry.
        pages cm
    ISBN 978-1-4556-1953-5 (hardcover : alk. paper) — ISBN 978-1-4556-1954-2 (e-book)
    1. Nursery rhymes, American. [1. New Orleans (La.)—Juvenile poetry.] I. Gentry,
    Marita, illustrator. II. Title.
    PS3601.D364N49 2014
    811'.6—dc23
                                                                    2014000157

Printed in Malaysia
Published by Pelican Publishing Company, Inc.
1000 Burmaster Street, Gretna, Louisiana 70053
www.pelicanpub.com

The King of France

The King of France
had a great chance
  to build a town with taste.

The sirs Bienville
and Iberville
  set out to build with haste.

  The brothers made,
  with tools and trade,
    a place of wondrous dreams.

  The king then cried,
  "I'm filled with pride!"
    And thus came New Orleans.

I Had a Li'l Pecan Tree

I had a li'l pecan tree—
grew nothing till July
but tiny silver trays
for sweet pecan pie.

The King of France's daughter
came to visit me.
I shared these treats with her
on the Mississippi.

Ring around the City

Ring around the Quarter,
a city by the water.
Tremé! Marigny!
We'll stay downtown.

Ring around the wharf plank,
from there we spy the Westbank.
Gretna, Algiers,
and back around!

Round and Round the Garden District

Round and round the
   Garden District
down Magazine Street:
architecture, tourist lectures,
   fair ladies we will greet.

Round and round the
   Garden District
giddy children roam.
River breeze, magnolia trees—
   they call the Crescent home.

Petit Jacques la Ronde

Petit Jacques la Ronde
on the neutral ground
of Decatur and Esplanade
found a Lucky Dog vendor
who said with great candor,
"I'll give you a dog that's homemade."

I-10

Treme

Louis
Armstrong
Park

N. Rampart St.

Esplanade Ave.

Marigny

Canal Street

Super Dome

French Quarter

LUCKY DOGS

Who Dat!

Jack Sprat

Jack Sprat, he yelled, "Who dat!"
riding on the *Creole Queen*,
for there's no better place to be
than down in New Orleans!

New Orleans, New Orleans

New Orleans, New Orleans,
has red and white and butter beans.
Ice cream for you, pralines for me,
to please the people of this city.
    So many choices one can test,
    but who can tell which they love best?

Creamy sno-balls we will savor,
of more than twenty-seven flavors!
There's nectar cream and tangerine
for the folks of New Orleans.
    So many choices one can test,
    but who can tell which they love best?

Red Beans

Red beans, sweet pralines,
ready for hungry folks.
Fill a plate—don't make 'em wait—
and sit by City Park oaks.

FRENCH MARKET

French Market, French Market

French Market, French Market,
  to buy a gris-gris charm.
Fell down there, oh *ma chère*,
  a cause for alarm!

French Market, French Market,
  peddlers tug at my arm.
Starts to rain, home again,
  to avoid more harm.

Li'l Chère Meunière

Li'l Chère Meunière
sat on her derrière
eating some beans and rice.
Along came a frog,
who hopped on a log,
and asked for her meal—with a price.

She scowled and said,
"Dumb frog, drop dead!"
I don't have enough for you too."
The toad cried in vain;
his hunger remained,
so he waved her a *mal adieu*.

Li'l Chère Meunière
stood in the air
and bumped her head on a tree.
She called, "What a brute
who sat on that root!"
and suddenly fell to her knees.

Little did Chère know,
next to her toe,
her guest had left a surprise.
It itched, it burned,
and red it turned,
and swelled to a really big size.

She ran like a faun
from Bayou St. John,
crying out for her mother's care.
For now it is clear
by that frog's souvenir
what happens to girls who don't share!

Jacques and Gilles

Jacques and Gilles climbed Monkey Hill
while visiting Audubon Zoo.
Jacques, he cried, "I want pecan pie!"
And Gilles agreed, "I do too."

Jacques and Gilles felt all their pockets
to see what change they had left.
Jacques looked ill, felt no crumpled bills,
and realized there was a great theft.

Jacques and Gilles left Monkey Hill
with a valuable lesson:
you must hold tight onto change that's light,
or you won't have it long (I'm just guessin')!

Ton, Ton, the Trumpeter's Son

Ton, Ton, the trumpeter's son
played some jazz on Rue Bourbon.
The crowd cried, "Mo'!
Let's fais do-do!"
So Ton played zydeco.

All around the Crescent City

All around the Vieux Carré,
locals hear the trumpet.
They stomp the floor and beg for more.
Brump! goes the trumpet.

Up and down St. Charles Avenue,
tourists board the streetcar.
Under the oaks ride all the folks.
Clang! goes the streetcar.

All around the stadium,
fans cheer the home team.
No more the 'Aints—we're proud of the Saints!
Who dat! for the home team.

Up and down the river chug
the ferry and the steamboat.
They turn—oh no! There's nowhere to go!
Crash! goes the steamboat!

Hey, Trumpet Player

Hey, trumpet player,
the fans said a prayer,
Reggie jumped over the goal.
The crowd held its breath
to see such a sight
as the Saints won a Super Bowl!

Carnival Is Coming

Carnival is coming;
Tuesday is getting fat.
Wear a pretty costume,
and grab an oyster sack.

If you haven't got an oyster sack,
a paper one will do.
It fills with throws so quickly,
'cause I can catch *beaucoup!*

Boys and Girls, Come Out to Play

Boys and girls, come out to play—
parades are rolling out today!
Eat your gumbo, move your feet
with New Orleanians in the street.
Doubloons from mid-air you snag
and scream, "Hey, mister!" to fill
    your bag.
Down St. Charles and up Canal,
we'll catch beads with high morale.
Gleeful merriment as we play—
laissez les bon temps rouler!

Sing a Song of Parades

Sing a song of parades,
a pocketful of beads,
catching all the doubloons
as the float proceeds.

When we scream "Hey, mister!"
revelers throw us more.
What shiny things we do take home
to use for fine décor!

We wake up in the morning
to see the Zulu Queen.
For those who catch a coconut,
it's luck that is foreseen.

When the day is over,
the masqueraders cheer—
can't wait for Fat Tuesday
to come again next year!

Old King Rex

Old King Rex was a giddy old man,
and a giddy old man was he.
He called to his court, and he called to his
    queen—
how lucky that man must be!

And every year, on Mardi Gras day,
he'd wave to all he meets.
He'd drink merrily and eat heartily,
as we all crowd into the street.

He sung out a phrase for all to hear:
"*Laissez-les bon temps rouler!*
I hope you have fun. Let the parade
    begin,
as we party till Ash Wednesday."

Old King Rex had a very good day,
a very good day indeed.
He ate crawfish bread then tucked into
    bed,
surrounded by Carnival beads.

One, Two

Un, deux,
délicieux!

Trois, quatre,
devant le théâtre . . .

cinq, six,
on mange une belle saucisse.

Sept, huit,
bon appétit,

   neuf, dix,
    Dieu bénisse!

Georgé Porgé

Georgé Porgé ate crab cakes,
saw one move, cried, "Heaven's
  sakes!"
When he found out the crab still
  lived,
His plate, he dropped—his face,
  he hid.

Jacques Be Nimble

Jacques be nimble,
Jacques be quick,
Jacques eats po' boys
till he gets sick.

Jacques be greedy,
which to test:
roast beef with gravy
or oysters, dressed?

Flaky Pastries

Flaky pastries sat on a plate;
Flaky pastries sealed their own fate.
  (All the cook's cousins and all the
    cook's friends
  asked for more, again and again.)

Mathieu, Marc, Luc, et Jean

Mathieu, Marc, Luc, et Jean
dressed the po' boy they ate
  on.
"Catfish or shrimp," they had
  said,
"Remoulade upon French
  bread!"
One half grilled, one half
  fried—
finished it quick? Boy, they
  tried!

The Baker and the Chef

The baker and the chef,
the baker and the chef.
Aiyee! A fleur-de-lis!
The baker and the chef.

The baker makes King Cake,
the baker makes King Cake.
Aiyee! A fleur-de-lis!
The baker makes King Cake.

Someone finds the baby,
someone finds the baby.
Aiyee! A fleur-de-lis!
Someone finds the baby.

The chef stirs a roux,
the chef stirs a roux.
Aiyee! A fleur-de-lis!
The chef stirs a roux.

The filé gumbo's ready,
the filé gumbo's ready.
Aiyee! A fleur-de-lis!
The filé gumbo's ready.

We eat up every drop,
we eat up every drop.
Aiyee! A fleur-de-lis!
We eat up every drop!

Peter, Peter, Gumbo Mixer

Peter, Peter, gumbo mixer,
Not so tasty, how to fix 'er?
Add an oyster, stir it well.
(Be sure to shuck it from its shell!)

Peter, Peter, gumbo saver,
add no more, your food we favor.
When it's cool, we'll want to eat.
Oh, what's better than a gumbo treat!

Yummy, Yummy, Pain Perdu

Yummy, yummy, pain perdu,
making you is no voodoo.
In my tummy you will be
like maque choux and andouille.
Yummy, yummy, pain perdu,
making you is no voodoo.

Yummy, yummy, pain perdu,
making you is no voodoo.
On the stovetop you will fry.
Serve it up with pecan pie.
Yummy, yummy, pain perdu,
call some friends, and share it, too.

Three Fat Chefs

Three fat chefs, three fat chefs:
see how they chop, see how they chop.
They all work with the sharpest knives
and fry up shrimp for their hungry wives.
Did you ever see such a sight in your life
as three fat chefs?

Three fat chefs, three chefs:
see how they stir, see how they stir.
They all add in andouille and rice;
if it burns they give it to the alley mice.
Did you ever see such a roll of the dice
as three fat chefs?

Three fat chefs, three fat chefs:
see how they eat, see how they eat.
On Royal Street they hungrily wail;
to drink they order a ginger ale.
For a good table they fight tooth and nail,
those three fat chefs!

Little Dolly Derbigny

Little Dolly Derbigny
sat in a park in Gentilly
bored completely out of her head.
Her mother yelled, "I declare!
Stand up and go play elsewhere!"
So she went downtown instead.

Little Dolly Derbigny
walked to the Faubourg Marigny
much to her delight and surprise.
She danced to the catchy beat
of music on Frenchmen Street
then left to see the moon rise.

Little Dolly Derbigny
sat on the wall of the levee
to watch the stars high in the sky.
She thought, as they did glimmer,
and as the night grew dimmer,
"Oh, what a spectacular day had I."

Marie, Marie, Quite Scary

Marie, Marie, quite scary,
how does your gris-gris work?
With voodoo dolls and quadroon balls
and mysteries that may lurk.

Down in Mid-City

Down in Mid-City,
it can be scary
with ghouls, ghosts, and tombs
in huge cemeteries.

Down in City Park,
it's spooky and dark—
I saw a full moon
and started to bark!

Danse pour Ton Papa

Danse pour ton papa
mon petit bébé!

Danse pour ta maman
mon petit bébé!

Danse pour tes amis
mon petit bébé!

Et danse pour tout le monde
tous les jours et toutes les nuits!

Lundi's Child

Lundi's child eats shrimp and rice.
Mardi's child is full of spice.
Mercredi's child plays zydeco.
Jeudi's child loves Satchmo mo'.
Vendredi's child makes shrimp boulette.
Samedi's child's from Lafayette.
But those born on dimanche, you know,
rest and relax and fais do-do!

Row, Row, Ton Bateau

Row, row *ton bateau*
up to New Orleans.
Merrily, merrily, merrily, merrily,
for rice and butter beans.

Row, row *ton bateau*
down Dulac today.
Merrily, merrily, merrily, merrily,
for crawfish étouffée.

Little Bayou

Little Bayou,
please fill with fish.
Keep us fed
with a deep-fried dish.

Where do you flow
if it starts to rain?
Into the lake
called Pontchartrain.

I would join you
with my boat of tin,
but I'd be afraid
of falling in!

Li'l Rideaux

Li'l Rideaux lost his *bateau*
and didn't know where to find it;
while doing the wash, it went with a *slosh*,
since he'd forgotten to bind it.

Li'l Rideaux cried "oh-my-yo!"
and searched his house and behind it.
With his hands all wet, he realized his *bête*,
gone from the dock he resigned it.

Later that day, the fishermen say,
Li'l Rideaux had been sobbing,
"Without my skiff, my life's adrift.
My line will never be bobbing!"

The Gulf wind heard, rose up and stirred
as Rideaux let daylight dim,
and then with a quiver, from up the river,
sailed a mighty ship just for him.

Li'l Boudreaux and Thibodaux

Li'l Boudreaux and Thibodaux
agreed to have a battle.
For Li'l Boudreaux said Thibodaux
broke his pirogue paddle.

Just then swam by a great redfish,
and as they fell back on their laurels,
"It's mine!" one said; the other, "You wish!"
thus starting back the quarrel.

The Mischievous Nutria

A trapper went boating upon the marsh land,
  varoomity-roomity-rump!
His daughter beside him held nets in her hand,
  merrily-errily-mump!

A nutria cried *Whank!* and they fell in the swamp,
  splishity-splashity-sploosh!
Both jumped up, enraged by the romp,
  wishity-washity-woosh!

The mischievous nutria swam swiftly away,
  swimity-swamity-swum!
and thought, "Not today! My fur you won't fray!
  I happily-appily won!"

What Are Little Creoles Made Of?

What are Creole girls made of?
  Sugared beignets and café au laits.
That's what Creole girls are made of.

What are Creole boys made of?
  Hubig's pies and Zatarain fries.
That's what Creole boys are made of.

Little Cajun Girl

I am a pretty little Cajun girl
from the town of Arabi.
All the fishermen on the docks
give me their fish for free.

My boyfriend's name is Nathan,
born on LeBeau Plantation
with okra for his toes and a muffuletta nose,
and that's the way my story goes.

There Was a Cajun Woman

There was a Cajun woman in a pirogue
who flew high in the sky with a cackle.
"It's suppertime," she rasped in a brogue
as she grasped a pole and some tackle.

"Old woman, old woman," I said as she flew,
"Why are you going so high?"
"To hook a starfish to put in my stew,
which I'll serve with chocolate moon pie!"

Rub-a-Dub-Dub

Rub-a-dub-dub,
three shrimp in a tub.
Which one do you think they'll eat?

The closest, the center?
Maybe not either!
But it certainly will not be me!

Ding Dong Bell

Ding dong bell,
a crawfish, by its smell.

Who put it in
from Plaquemine?

Who pulled it out?
My old dog Scout.

(He has one big wish:
to eat crawfish!)

But my dog, he flinched
when the crawfish pinched!

Eency Weency Crawfish

Eency weency crawfish
crawled out the bayou's end.
Out came the shrimp nets
and caught up all his friends.

Up came his mother,
who warned "Don't be insane!"
So the eency weency crawfish
turned back around again.

Pelican, Pelican

Pelican, pelican,
Where'd you fly a while?
Down to the Gulf of Mexico
next to Grand Isle.

Pelican, pelican,
what did you do there?
I stole all the fish from
the fishermen's ware.

Natchez

I had a little dog and called him Natchez.
He ate hot sauce and lit up like matches.
I sent him up the bayou with a big crab trap.
He caught up a dozen with a little lagniappe.

I sent him to the market to fetch plantains.
He returned with Tabasco 'cause he wasn't
    restrained.
I sent him out west to Avery Isle.
Red peppers he saw and started to smile.

It's Raining, It's Pouring

It's raining, it's pouring,
the French Quarter's flooding.
Flood gates open, water's out!
Now it's high and dry again.

The Gulf Wind Does Blow

The Gulf wind does blow—
it's a hurricane!
And what will the Cajuns do,
poor things?

They'll hide shuttered in
and wait yet again
till the land is all dry,
poor things.

Causeway Bridge

Causeway Bridge has fallen down, fallen down, fallen down.
Causeway Bridge has fallen down, my fair mayor.

Give it love and patch it up, patch it up, patch it up.
Give it love and patch it up, my fair mayor.

We can cross it once it's safe, once it's safe, once it's safe.
We can cross it once it's safe, my fair mayor.

Causeway Bridge is now fixed up, now fixed up, now fixed up.
Causeway Bridge is now fixed up—thanks, fair mayor!

'Tite Pattie Pinkie

'Tite Pattie Pinkie jams through the town,
on stage, off stage, in a ball gown.
Tapping to a drum beat, singing at the mic,
we'll be dancing here for as long as you like.

Hey, Pattie Pinkie, where you singing at?
Down in the Quarter, or at the Spotted Cat?
Dancers dance all around, outside the cars go *beep!*
Play if you must, we will never fall asleep.

Anything you play, jazz girl, don't stop until it's sunny;
we love your singing voice, as sweet as golden honey.
Your look and song is classic for the old and young,
belting tunes we all adore in your Cajun tongue.

Hey, Pattie Pinkie, the children all cry,
You're glistening stardust in everyone's eye.
Though a storm's a-brewing and we feel the rain drop,
please, Pattie Pinkie, don't ever, ever stop!

Lucky is the listener whose ears will fall on you,
as no one sings a melody as well as you can do.
To lovers of New Orleans, you open up your door
with a kiss of jazz for those who'll enjoy it more.

One, Two

One, two,
boogaloo;

three, four,
Saints fans roar;

five, six,
beignet mix;

seven, eight,
evacuate . . .

nine, ten,

Come
back
again!

Author's Note

The marriage between New Orleans and the nursery rhyme was inevitable. Both radiate a sort of infinite, timeless magic. It's no surprise to see an attraction such as Storyland in our own City Park, juxtaposed among the ancient oaks since the 1950s, displaying the various nursery rhyme characters that we know and cherish.

Nursery rhymes hold an innate versatility that helps the reader to sing along or fill in his or her own words to personalize it with a favorite memory, feeling, city, or region. The familiarity of New Orleans iconology and the simplicity of the nursery rhyme lend themselves to this sort of poetry gumbo. One of my first memories of the French Quarter is of strolling down Bourbon Street in midday and seeing a young Creole lady singing her heart out to a jazzy tune. I merged that memory with the classic rhyme "Wee Willie Winkie" and created "'Tite Pattie Pinkie." The cadence of the original rhyme is there, but the story is mine.

Mixing my favorite city with my favorite nursery rhymes was a reflective exercise on my part, and I enjoyed every minute of it. Go on, now you try one!